SECRETS OF A WELL DRESSED BRAND

THE ART OF INCREASING YOUR PERCEIVED VALUE

Toi Sweeney

WHAT OTHERS ARE SAYING

"THE REAL DEAL"

GINA GROVE

Many people claim to be stylsts and image consultants. The real deal is with Toi Sweeney, not only a genuine person but examines one's lifestyle to help master their brand. This book is a must buy, easy to read, great tips and suggestions for anyone wanting to take their personal brand to the utmost level.

"TRANSFORMATIVE LOOK AT THE POWER OF STYLE"

ISIS SMALLS

The wisdom and insights in this book has seriously enhanced the quality of my life. Before reading this book, I disliked shopping with a passion. I was completely overwhelmed by the idea of putting together a stylish look and I honestly devalued the power of "dressing for success." However, in my profession as a public speaker, how I dress is key to my brand.

Toi's "secrets" helped me realize that my outfit speaks before I even open my mouth. From the advice to the discovery quizzes, this book is power-packed with practical, easy-to-understand ways to discover your brand and build a closet that reflects it. And, it's incredibly inspirational! It gave me a deeper motivation for discovering my style.

I now feel more confident and I actually look forward to building my closet with clothes that reflect me and what I value. I have cut my shopping time in half and I have learned how to dress in a way that is strategic and effective for not only my speaking engagements, but my everyday life.

"THE DEFINITIVE GUIDE FOR PERSONAL STYLE"

RYAN RHOTEN

Before you ever say a verbal word to someone you're about to meet, you've already said volumes to them via your clothes. Toi is an expert helping you say the right things through your personal style. Way more than a how-to-dress book, Secrets of a Well Dressed Brand is the definitive guide on how to use the most visible part of your brand to set the stage for your success.

"SET YOURSELF APART"

CHRISTI MIRANDA

This book is easy to read & apply immediately! It's packed full with action steps to really set you apart. The interviews with other experts were a surprise bonus. I am more confident now on honing in on my own style brand! I will reference this book again & again.

"NOT WHAT YOU THINK"

STEVE RISINGER

This book is NOT about materialism! Toi gets to the heart behind the decisions you're making and teaches mental discipline regarding wardrobe. She is placing tools in your hands that will set you up for being able to impact the world best with your gifts and talents.

"PROCEED WITH CAUTION"

JASON CRUISE

In all sincerity, I had an incredibly hard time making the phone call to Toi about personal style. I'm not one to value material things, while at the same time, there's just no way around it: people make character assessments based on how you look and appear in public.

The reason I say, "Proceed With Caution" is because you're going to re-think a lot about what you wear after you read this book. I did most certainly.

Toi's approach on personal style that comes up, or through, what you wear is something that was revolutionary for me. It steered the idea far from fashion, and placed the focus where it should be, on your personal brand and the style that makes that brand consistent.

She taught me that your core values, what makes "you, the you you are" is shown through how you dress. Your dress is a refelection of "who" you are and "what" you value.

"TAKE IT TO THE NEXT LEVEL"

RISExLA ATTENDEE

I heard Toi Sweeney speak at RISExLA in 2018. Her clothes and shoe game is on point. I purchased this book to see how I could build my own personal brand to set myself apart from the crowd and get noticed in my industry.

Toi has assembled everything you need to take it to the next level. I wish I had found this book sooner, but better late than never.

Secrets of a Well-Dressed Brand

Copyright © 2022 Toi Sweeney

Fifth Anniversary Edition

www.ToiSweeney.com

Copyright protects the voice of the author, encourages diversity of thought, creates space for uninhibited creativity, and adds value to the human experience. Thank you for buying this book and thereby promoting free speech. No portion of this book may be reproduced mechanically, electronically, or by any other means, including photocopy, without permission of the publisher or author except in the case of brief quotations embodied in critical articles and reviews. It is illegal to copy this book, post it to a website, or distribute by any other means without permission from the publisher/author.

The purpose of this book is to educate and inspire as a work of creative nonfiction. The author and/or publisher shall have neither liability nor responsibility to anyone with respect to any loss or damage caused, or alleged to be caused, directly or indirectly by the information contained in this book. The experiences and words are the author's alone.

Cover Design and Formatting: Meg Delagrange-Belfon

ISBN: 979-8-9856124-7-9

PRINTED IN THE UNITED STATES OF AMERICA

CONTENTS

29   **CHAPTER ONE**
YOU ARE A PRODUCT:
PERSONAL BRANDING 101

43   **CHAPTER TWO**
HOW DOES YOUR BRAND IMPACT OTHERS?

57   **CHAPTER THREE**
THE POWER OF PERCEIVED VALUE

67   **CHAPTER FOUR**
THE AMAZING IMPACT OF STYLE

95   **CHAPTER FIVE**
HOW TO BECOME A WELL-DRESSED BRAND

111   **CHAPTER SIX**
HOW TO CREATE A BRAND-RIGHT CLOSET

121   **CHAPTER SEVEN**
DO YOU NEED AN IMAGE CONSULTANT
OR FASHION STYLIST?

133   **CHAPTER EIGHT**
PUTTING IT ALL TOGETHER

143   **CHAPTER NINE**
PRACTICE MAKES BETTER

GUEST INTERVIEWS

- MARCUS ALLEN
- STEPHANIE HUMPHREY
- JESSE GARZA & JOE LUPO
- ANNE EWERS
- JIM BRACELIN

RYAN RHOTEN

OWNER AT **THE DISTILLED BRAND**

FORWARD

"Clothes are your packaging."

My mind was blown right then and there. Fortunately, Toi continued her answer so I could take a few seconds to absorb the words I'd just heard. *Clothes are your packaging.*

As simple as that sounds, this was a revelation for me. I'd always known clothes were important, but I had never considered them to be an integral part of my brand. (More on that in a minute.)

After our interview, as I reflected on the content in the show, I knew it would change my thoughts on style, image, and personal branding forever.

Thinking back now as I write these words, I don't remember exactly how Toi and I met. Twitter, I think. (It must have been Twitter, because I remember that she took the time to have a conversation with me, as opposed to just coming out and asking to be a guest on the podcast like many others do.)

As we "spoke," I found myself more and more intrigued with her comments and views on personal branding. I knew I had to have her on the show. After we scheduled our time for the interview, I remember thinking to myself two things. First, who is Toi really, and second, what do clothes have to do with personal branding? As it turns out, a lot.

I think anyone who speaks with Toi for the first time will come away with two things. First, Toi knows her stuff. She has over twenty years of hands-on experience in the fashion industry as a brand image strategist, and a successful entrepreneur. Her accolades include being featured on TV and in print publications such as TEDx , Where Women Work Magazine, and The Philadelphia Inquirer. She's even won the prestigious Telly Award.

While her accomplishments and awards are an external visualization of her success in her field, the second and most important thing you'll notice about Toi when you meet her for the first time is her commitment and passion to helping professionals get on the pathway to a more confident and coordinated appearance.

She does this by matching your style with your brand. In other words, she doesn't try to change who you are. Instead, she works with you to build a brand that accentuates and helps to tell your individual story in a manner which is consistent with who you are already.

When working with Toi, you learn very quickly that she doesn't dwell on the possibilities of "fine," and she challenges you to do the same. Toi knows that when you look good, you feel good. And if you feel good, you gain confidence.

Think about the last time you had to "dress up" for an event, a gala, a dance, a business meeting, or an interview. How did you feel? If you're like me, you felt more alive and more confident. Maybe you walk a little taller or you feel a little stronger. Would you like to feel that way more often? This is the feeling Toi helps her clients achieve every day.

Back to this concept of clothes being your packaging. Take a minute to consider this scenario: You are shopping for a new computer. On the shelf in front of you are two boxes—packages, if you will—containing new computers. Before you dive into the specifications and functionality of each, you notice differences right away.

One box is white, clean and shrink-wrapped. You can tell, without picking it up, that the package is sturdy and clean. There are very few markings on the package; it seems pure and complete. Almost like it was made just for you.

The other box is the color of cardboard because that is what it is. There is no shrink-wrap on this package, and it has many markings and labels on it. It feels like it was put there on the shelf by the delivery driver. It appears to have been made for anyone.

If you had to choose one and only by its appearance, which would you choose?

While clearly not a clothing scenario, keep in mind that both packages tell a story, and that story is communicated to you in in as little as one-tenth of a second. That's how long it takes us as humans to subconsciously determine things such as product quality.

Your clothes are no different. In that same one-tenth of a second, we all judge each other on whether or not we think someone is likable, of high status, or maybe even a bit promiscuous. In the blink of an eye, we decide if someone is a perfectionist or more utilitarian. Toi understands the clothing you choose to wear helps to tell your story on the outside, and can position you for success in the eyes of others. Is your positioning that of a perfectionist, or is it more utilitarian?

Consider this scenario: Two people are sitting in a reception area. Both are waiting to be interviewed for the same position.

One candidate is wearing a blue business suit with matching accessories. The other candidate is wearing jeans with a blouse and blazer. If you were interviewing these two, which one would you give the nod to before they even spoke their first words?

This is the power of your clothes. They can be like the bow on the car in the Lexus commercials. Toi believes your packaging is one of the most visible ways for you to stand out from your competition. When your clothes compliment your brand and emphasize your story, they have the power to fascinate. Leveraging her Fascination Advantage® certifica-

FORWARD //

tion, Toi helps you understand how the world see you because in her eyes, your superpower is your product, and your product is your brand. Your superpower is, therefore, on display to others in what you say, what you do, and what you wear. It shows up in the colors you choose, the shoes you wear, and even how you wear your hair. It all leads back to your personal brand.

So how do you want to position yourself? What do you want your brand to say to others before you even speak a single word?

Toi has taken all her years of experience in image, style, and branding, and put them all in this book to help you answer these very important questions—questions whose answers can mean the difference between building your brand and positioning yourself for success, or constraining your brand and masking who you truly are.

As you read through the pages in this book, keep in mind that your clothes are your packaging. When they enhance and compliment your brand, they give you confidence. And with the right amount of confidence, the world can be yours.

    This book will show you the way.

TOI SWEENEY

CEO OF **THE WELL DRESSED BRAND**

INTRODUCTION

My name is Toi Sweeney, and I help turn anxiety into confidence. How? By guiding you to exceptional style. Why? Because if I were to take a look at what you are wearing right now, I would've already summed up your brand—and chances are, you could do a better job of looking the part.

Why? Looking the part will add to your perceived value, build your confidence, and allow you to run your company or excel at your job without having to worry about whether you are sending the right message.

One of the most challenging tasks that I faced while writing this book was deciding exactly what this book should be about. For the last few years, I've had such a strong focus on the image perspective of personal branding, mainly because my entire career has been about fashion and how to market it, sell it, and make it visually appealing to others.

> Are you sending the right message?

I also noticed that whenever I would read a book, listen to a podcast, or speak with someone about personal branding, the image aspect was rarely addressed. At best, it was mentioned in addition to a long list of things that you need to do to build your personal brand. I felt myself always wanting to interrupt the person being interviewed and take a deeper dive into image.

HOW I BECAME A WELL-DRESSED BRAND

(AND WHY I CAN HELP YOU!)

It has been said that it takes 10,000 hours of deliberate practice to become world-class in any field. When I think about it, I have 262,800 hours in the fashion industry and 87,600 hours dedicated to personal branding, specializing in the role that your image plays.

I began my career working in leadership roles for various retail companies. My introduction into the luxury market was working for Bloomingdale's in New York and going through their executive training program. I have always loved the luxury market, so I felt right at home getting to learn what it takes to become a luxury brand. I excelled in those roles and won various customer service awards.

My love of personal branding came while working at the nation's #1 home shopping channel. Halfway through my nearly 15 years at this company, I began to feel stuck. I was still grieving the loss of my first child and working on rebuilding my marriage. My evening wear design business had collapsed, and I felt as if I might, too.

As I clung to my faith like a child watching their first horror movie, I desperately needed to know what was next. I was overweight. I was sad. There was no upward mobility that existed for my current role as a fashion stylist.

I desperately wanted and needed to move forward.

I made a choice that, no matter how bad things were, I was going to win! I decided that I wanted to be exceptional in all facets of fashion styling.

I sat down and made a list of all the things that I wanted to do better. I listed everything from color combinations to accessorizing. I studied articles and magazines, read books—you name it! People began to notice.

Eventually, I learned that, a few months prior, I had been passed up for a chance to work on two of the top fashion shows that the company had to offer. I was in shock! I was a much better stylist than the person who was currently working on the show. I couldn't believe it.

Later that year, the truth about why I was passed over for the promotion was revealed. It was simple: I did not look the part. Because I did not look the part, the program host could not believe that I was a great stylist. She could only judge me by the brand message I was putting out there. She was right: I did not look like an exceptional stylist.

No one wants to be rejected, and I am no different. I decided that if I was going to proudly call myself a fashion stylist, I needed to look like one. After a few years of feeling sad, I did not want people thinking of me as a sad person. I lost about 25 pounds, and I looked great! (The purpose was not about being skinny; I wanted to be healthy because I was expecting a beautiful little boy via surrogacy and I wanted to ensure I was my best self for my family.)

I was finally starting to feel happy, too. I began playing with color and using the meaning behind specific colors to express how happy I was. People began telling me, "It is always a pleasure to see you! You look so happy."

It took some time, but I finally landed the position as a stylist for some new shows that were airing, including one of the highest-grossing nighttime fashions shows on this network! This platform allowed me to test my theories about the psychology of color and using clothing to tell a story. I added elements of each model's personal brand into each look, wondering if my ideas would translate on television. It worked!

Each week, the looks that I created for the company's website doubled in revenue. Next, I was promoted to a senior styling position, where I had the pleasure of supporting and managing the brand images of nearly 30 program hosts. I am forever grateful for this opportunity and the lessons that I had a chance to learn.

Today, I am the CEO of The Well-Dressed Brand, where I help each client become an exceptionally-styled, luxury brand. It is my greatest intention for this book to provide you with a paradigm shift in the way you choose to get dressed every day. I want you to be clear about your brand message and the importance of dressing your message.

Welcome to my deeper dive! Enjoy the journey.

Love ya!

Tori Sweeney

CHAPTER ONE

YOU ARE A PRODUCT

PERSONAL BRANDING 101

BEING A PRODUCT INVOLVES YOUR WHOLE SELF. WHEN YOU PACKAGE AND MARKET YOURSELF OR YOUR CAREER, YOU ARE CREATING A PERSONAL BRAND.

In 1997, when Tom Peters coined the phrase "personal branding," the overall concept was about self-packaging and marketing ourselves using the same tools large brands use to market their products. He provided the golden ticket, saying, "We are the CEOs of our own companies: Me, Inc. To be in business today, our most important job is to be head

marketer of the brand called you." Today, being chief marketer of your own brand is still relevant. But you must accept the fact that you are a product. Being a product involves your whole self. When you package and market yourself or your career, you are creating a personal brand. Your personal brand is made up of all the following things working together:

YOU ARE A PRODUCT: PERSONAL BRANDING 101

PERSONALITY

THE COLLECTION OF YOUR QUALITIES.
(THIS ALLOWS YOUR BRAND TO STAND OUT!)

CORE VALUES

THE GUIDING PRINCIPLES THAT
DICTATE YOUR BEHAVIORS AND ACTIONS.

MISSION

YOUR IMPORTANT GOAL OR PURPOSE,
ACCOMPANIED BY STRONG CONVICTIONS.

VISION

SOMETHING EVIDENT ABOUT YOU
THAT OTHERS CAN SENSE OR UNDERSTAND.

IMAGE

YOUR APPEARANCE AND
WHAT IT REFLECTS (LIKE A LIKENESS).

Your personal brand should answer the following questions:

- Who are you?
- What do you do?
- How do you add or create value?
- What makes you different than other professionals in your industry?
- How should you package your brand?
- What should your wear?
- What impression do you want to make when you enter a room?
- What do you want people to say about you when you leave a room?

YOU ARE A PRODUCT: PERSONAL BRANDING 101

WHY IS PERSONAL BRANDING IMPORTANT?

On a cold day in the Bronx in 1939, Jewish immigrants Frieda and Frank Lifshitz gave birth to their third child. They called him Ralph.

By age 16, Ralph was known for having a great sense of style and an eye for both fashion and business. I can only imagine that being teased about his calling card in life was not exactly a confidence booster. Ralph was very much aware of how he was being perceived, and he understood the impact that this could have on his future.

Setting his sights on a college education with the hope of building a men's wear line, he changed his last name to Lauren. Today, Ralph Lauren is one of the greatest American designers; his company's net worth stands at about $7.1 billion.

I once heard him say in an interview that he changed his name because no one was going to buy ties from Ralph Lifshitz. Personal branding and first impressions go hand-in-hand. The goal is to make a great first impression that will last.

Ralph Lauren was ahead of his time; he was the chief marketer of his own personal brand. He stood tall in the world by creating a company around his brand. Today, Ralph Lauren is a household name. There are 470, 892 people named Ralph in the U.S. There is only *one* Ralph Lauren.

We see the same strategy put into practice with singer and songwriter, Lizzo, whose birth name is Melissa Viviane Jefferson. According to Google, there are 771,433 people named Melissa is U.S. However, there is only *one* Lizzo.

Too many entrepreneurs, CEOs, and other leaders today miss the mark on this lesson. Having a personal brand as a leader is vital–end of story. Research conducted by Burson-Marsteller found that 48 percent of a company's reputation is directly determined by the public's perception of the CEO.

We're not shocked, right? People don't trust companies; they trust people. People don't leave companies; they leave leaders. As a leader, having a strong personal brand will allow you to attract top employees, great customers, friends, and fans!

A personal brand sets you apart as an expert in your industry. It allows you to help others through your successes and your failures, and to share your passion, mission, and vision along the way. Your personal brand writes the story of your core values, clearly communicating what you stand for and how you create value.

Finally, having a personal brand today helps you to control first impressions and negative perceptions. What you do for a living, in most cases, is a commodity—but you are unique.

There are many American designers. Fundamentally, they all do the same job. But again, there is only *one* Ralph Lauren.

Regardless of what you do for a living, there will

always be someone riding your coat tails who is more educated and has more money, better connections, and better ideas. The good news is... there is only one *you*!

You are the foundation of your brand. Personal branding is built on who you are, not what you do. Could there have been Apple without Steve Jobs?

You are the greatest asset to your business and your career. Why? Because the value is coming from you, not from the product or your company.

In the next chapter, we'll dig deeper into how your brand affects those around you. (*Hint: it's more impactful than you think!*)

In preparing for this book, I had the pleasure of sitting down to interview influential leaders from various backgrounds. Marcus Allen, the CEO of Big Brothers, Big Sisters, is one such example.

Let's look at why Marcus believes personal branding is important.

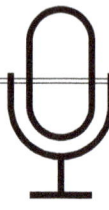

INTERVIEW

MARCUS ALLEN

CEO OF **BIG BROTHERS, BIG SISTERS**

"YOU NEED TO BRING VALUE ABOVE AND BEYOND WHAT'S ON YOUR RESUME." —MARCUS ALLEN

HOW WOULD YOU DESCRIBE YOUR PERSONAL BRAND?

Outside of my work ethic and my process is how I carry myself. It's not just what I dress like, but my presence. I believe that one of the best ways to ensure a successful career is to build your personal brand, because your personal brand works for you, even when you're asleep.

People have come to me and they say things like, "I ran into this person that knows you. And they're like, *Marcus is awesome. He's this, he's that...*"

Meanwhile, I'd be sitting there thinking, *I've never met that person. I don't know that person, that person don't know me. But they've heard someone else say something great about me.*

You have to manage your personal brand. And what I want my personal brand to stand for is consistency, someone who's professional, someone who serves others, and someone who helps people around him to have a good time.

It could be as simple as smiling a lot. I have [a quote] on my page that says, "Your smile is your personal brand". My smile is my personal logo. I smile every time I meet someone.

My grandma used to talk about how big my teeth are, and they used to call me horse when I was growing up. I turned my smile into an asset when I took every opportunity to show those big pearly whites.

So, when I look at my brand, and I continue to hone in and work on my brand. I try to ensure that certain things come to mind when people think of me.

HOW DO YOU HELP PEOPLE AS A LEADER?

I'm always trying to make sure the people that work for me get a chance to take advantage of opportunities, even if that means that they're going to leave our organization and go on to the next one. My job as a leader is not to build people to keep them loyal to me in this organization. My job is to help people become better. And by helping them become better, I help the community at large.

WHAT ARE SOME CHALLENGES THAT YOU FACE?

It's been a little difficult to develop a strong personal brand, because it's different when you're in the nonprofit realm. When you're creating a personal brand in a nonprofit career versus entrepreneurship or corporate, no one wants you to be [too flashy].

The understanding is that since we're all about doing good work, we should stay under the radar, and we shouldn't talk about it.

My response to that is, "Well, how am I going to raise money if nobody knows what we're doing? And how am I going to raise money, if people don't know who the leader is?"

People need to know our mission, they need to see the value or outcomes, and they also need to know who the leader is. People need to know the leader is reliable, to make sure that that he or she performs the mission. And it also helps a little bit if they like you, right? Just a little bit.

And so, my personal brand is one that I think some are getting used to in the nonprofit world because I do hear people talk about it. Some say I'm a self-promoter. Self-promoter is the negative connotation of building a personal brand, right? But for me, I've never seen anything wrong with being a self-promoter.

I'm hopeful that personal branding will catch on more with people in the nonprofit space, in the sense that you need to have bring value above and beyond your resume. You need to bring value with you above and beyond your work efforts that you're going to do at a particular company.

When I find people with personal brands that are known to get stuff done, they're known to be in certain circles, and they're known to accomplish expectations or goals, then those are the people that I want working for me. Having a personal brand is critical to what I do both in the nonprofit world, and in my entrepreneurial work.

CHAPTER TWO

HOW DOES YOUR BRAND IMPACT OTHERS?

MAKING SURE YOU HAVE A PERSONAL BRAND THAT TRULY SPEAKS TO WHO YOU ARE WILL POSITIVELY IMPACT EVERYONE AROUND YOU.

What if I told you that the human attention span is dwindling? OK—you're pretty smart, so most likely, you're not shocked.

But what if I told you that the human attention span is currently hovering at eight glorious seconds?

And…that the attention span of a goldfish is nine seconds? You walk into the room, we shake hands, and boom! You've been gold-fished. I'm already bored with your brand.

First impressions today are harder than ever, according to a study completed by Microsoft in 2015. Thanks to technology, our attention spans have dropped by four seconds since 2000.

We finally got this multitasking thing down, due in large part to our smart devices, but we now have the attention spans of a goldfish!

This eight-second world we live in is pretty scary when you think about it! In eight seconds, someone is deciding whether you are:

- **LIKABLE**
- **TRUSTWORTHY**
- **PROMISCUOUS**
- **HANDSOME**
- **BEAUTIFUL**
- **LOYAL**
- **SMART**

Then, they're off to the next thing before you get to make the right first impression! It's hard not to be distracted. (As I write this, I am quoting the scene from the movie Up: "Hi! My name's Doug. Will you be my master? SQUIRREL!" That's pretty much what the world is like.)

Your personal brand needs staying power, whether someone is meeting you for the first time or scrolling through your social media posts. You can't build a relationship or tell someone who you are and what you do in 8 seconds! Your personal brand has to do the work for you.

Making sure you have a personal brand that truly speaks to who you are will positively impact everyone around you. The key is not getting distracted. In this noisy world, that may seem impossible.

Stay focused on your goals, your values, and your mission. Use your personality to dress the part. Why?

Because at some point, we all have to step out from behind our computers and meet clients. What you wear to those meetings can make or break a deal in just a few seconds. The visual aspect of your personal brand speaks volumes instantly.

PAJAMAS? ...REALLY?!

I was reading a story the other day about a headmistress of a school in London who sent letters home with her students, asking the parents not to wear their pajamas when they picked their kids up from school. And a judge in New Jersey posted signs in his courtroom, asking people to please not wear pajamas into court.

I get it: we have become a culture of casual dressers, comfy clothes, and lounge wear. Pajamas have become the clothing of choice for dropping kids off at school, airports, and, in some cases, a day in court.

So, if people already have a perception of you, you already have a brand. They're saying good or bad things about you when you're not in the room: "She/

he always looks put together," or, "He/she looks like they just rolled out of bed."

You get to decide whether your standard of dress will ride alongside the pajama wearers, or if you're willing to raise the bar on your personal brand by setting a new standard!

I am not suggesting that you wear a 3-piece suit every day, especially if your workplace is casual. (But in a room full of khaki and blue shirts, you will stand out.) I am not suggesting that you dress up in your favorite couture item and sing Iggy Azalea lyrics ("I'm so fan-seh!"). I am, however, here to remind you that you have a choice.

When you look good, you feel good. When you feel good, you are confident. When you are confident, the world is yours.

When you look the part, other people begin to notice. When you don't look the part, you stand out for all the wrong reasons.

Every time you get dressed or post something online, I want you to consider your image, your personality, your core values, your mission, and your vision. This will ensure you are staying on track with your brand (and it cuts down on the bad outfit days!). Your personal brand will help you stay true to who you are and become the person of influence you're striving to be.

Later in the book, we will hone in on how the world sees you. We'll talk about how creating a brand identity and a brand mantra will help you stand out on social media, and much more!

It's amazing how much your appearance influences others' opinion of you. That's their first impression of your brand. You want your look to hit the nail on the head, every time.

In the next chapter, we'll focus on the power of perceived value. Your image communicates your value. We'll talk about how that translates into positioning yourself as a luxury brand, and demanding that others see you that way.

LOOKING THE PART MAKES A DIFFERENCE

Stephanie Humphrey is a television personality and tech expert. She's a regular on Harry and has appeared on many major networks. I am lucky enough to have her as a client and as a friend. Together, we have been able to make some killer first impressions by making sure she always looks the part.

On the next page, learn how personal branding has made a difference for Stephanie.

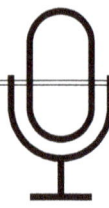

INTERVIEW

STEPHANIE HUMPHREY

TECHNOLOGY & LIFESTYLE CONTRIBUTOR AT **ABC NEWS MAKING TECH EASIER FOR ALL OF US WITH THE #60SECONDTECHBREAK** | AUTHOR | PROFESSIONAL SPEAKER AT **'TIL DEATH DO YOU TWEET** | TEDX SPEAKER

"YOU NEVER GET A SECOND CHANCE TO MAKE A FIRST IMPRESSION." - STEPHANIE HUMPHREY

FIRST, TELL US ABOUT YOURSELF!

My name is Stephanie Humphrey and I'm your friendly neighborhood tech life expert. Basically, what I do is show people how technology makes their lives easier. Very, very simple.

I got into it, not by accident because nothing happens by accident, but I was an engineer for 13 years and took a little bit of a detour into the entertainment industry. I did a little bit of modeling, a little bit of acting, and a little bit of hosting.

I decided that I wanted to marry my passion, which was technology with all of that newfound media training that I had gotten over the course of several years. So, a tech life expert was born and a brand was born, back in 2011. I've been working that brand ever since.

HOW WOULD YOU DESCRIBE YOUR PERSONAL BRAND?

I would describe my personal brand as smart and cool. I'm not looking to be that stereotypical "tech person", but I am a geek. I'm a proud nerd and I embrace that fully. But I don't necessarily think you need to actually look like that archetype to be taken seriously as a tech expert. If you can marry the idea of someone who is smart, someone who is forward thinking, and someone who is trendy with the idea that you can also still be very cool, chic, fashionable, and stylish — I think that's where you get me.

HOW IMPORTANT IS IMAGE TO YOUR PERSONAL BRAND?

I have two stories that celebrate, if you will, how important image is to my personal brand.

One is relative to the ensemble that I'm wearing for this interview. I can remember when this look first got put together. I loved it immediately. We know it worked — it communicated that quintessential epitome of smart and cool!

Soon after, I had an interview in New York. On the 75-yard walk from where I was parked to the building where I was going, no fewer than three people stopped to tell me they loved my outfit, saying the skirt I was wearing was *everything*.

Clothing makes a difference. When random strangers notice how well put together you are, it gives you confidence. It definitely made my back a bit straighter that day as I walked into the audition.

The person who was running everything greeted me and also noticed what I was wearing, complimenting me on my skirt. Showing up well-dressed checked boxes that I didn't have to prove later on. Making an excellent first impression was already out of the way.

When you are well dressed, it does so much for you. When you show up for an interview, you already have to worry about what you're going to say and how you're going to portray yourself. You may wonder whether you have all your content or you may worry whether you've hit all your talking points.

You don't want to have to worry about whether you looked good, whether it was appropriate, or whether you are portraying the image that they are looking for. To be well-dressed means that you get to focus on what you do best and that is invaluable.

In my second example, I had a meeting with a potential agent. What I've learned in this process is that less is usually more. Sometimes all it takes is that one signature piece to make the right statement without speaking loudly.

On this particular day, I was dressed simply, with a fabulous gray jacket that was the centerpiece of the entire look — simple, classy, sporty elegance.

During my interview at this high-end agency, I received at least four compliments on my jacket. I began to wonder if the compliments would translate into being signed with this agency, and I was! I did end up working with that agency.

The point is that they did recognize the effort and the thought that was put into my look that day. My clothing made a difference. Even though it was a simple outfit with a gray jacket, the intentionality of how the look was put together really made a difference. It made a difference in how I felt as I spoke during my interview. It made a difference in our connection.

When people appreciate how you present your

brand image, it creates a level of trust and instant connection between you. Within seconds, you've already brought so much to the table. Obviously, you have to back that up with good content and talent and a great personality, but your first impression is already done. You never get a second chance to make a first impression.

CHAPTER THREE

THE POWER OF PERCEIVED VALUE

HOW YOU PRESENT YOURSELF SPEAKS TO THE EXPECTATION AND THE PERCEIVED VALUE OF YOUR BRAND.

We are all in sales, selling our products, services, or just selling ourselves. Dictionary.com offers this definition of selling: "to cause to be accepted, especially generally or widely." We all want to be accepted.

Businesses cannot move forward without sales. In order for your customers to buy, they must perceive a value in what you're selling, meaning they must perceive a value in you.

I am inspired by the work of Brian Wansink, a professor at Cornell University. Wansink has made it part of his life's work to study how perceived value motivates behavior. Through his work, we've learned that perceived value is a powerful motivator in how people will perceive your personal brand.

Wansink conducted a test where consumers were served chocolate cake. The cake was served to the first group on a napkin; the second group received

the cake on a paper plate. The cake was served to the third group on Wedgwood china.

It's hard to deny the power of perception when you review the results. The first group–let's call them the napkin eaters–thought the cake was good. The second group, the paper plate eaters, thought the cake was great.

But the third group, who received their cake on china, not only thought the cake was amazing–they were also willing to pay triple the amount.

LEVEL-UP YOUR PRESENTATION

Just like the slice of cake served on fine china, how you present yourself speaks to the expectation and the perceived value of your brand.

About seven years ago, my husband, John, was

contacted by a recruiter at work who was looking for a new regional sales manager for a client. After they chatted for a while, John let the recruiter know that he did not know of anyone who could fill the position. The recruiter kindly asked him if he was interested, and if so, he just passed his phone interview!

John agreed to send him his resume so they could move on to the second round of the interview. There was only one problem: John had never interviewed for a job in his life! At age 17, he asked his parents to sign him into the Marine Corps. When he decided to leave the Marines after 10 years, all other jobs he received came from word of mouth, his reputation, and his employers' reliance on his personal brand to hold true.

I'll never forget the response from the recruiter once he learned this information: "You've never had a job interview? Now…either you're just that good, or really bad!"

As John was moving on to his third round of interviews—the face-to-face round—we never lost sight of the fact that there are expectations and perceived value. John, of course, did not disappoint.

Later, we found out that the executives were not only impressed with John; they also could not get over how well-dressed he was for the interview. When everyone else showed up in khakis and polo shirts—the equivalent of a paper plate—he arrived in a suit. *Hello, Wedgwood china!* This made an impression, and I'm happy to report that he was offered the job.

John had already built a personal brand around being an excellent leader. His background in the military, along with being a tour manager for some pretty major celebrities, is very impressive. He is very likable and charming; however, at that time, he was invisible on all digital platforms. You could not Google him. You couldn't find him on LinkedIn, which means that he had to lead with an exceptional personal brand to knock out the competition.

John was very lucky that the recruiter looks for special people who are not on social media. Personal branding is emotional; it can influence how people feel. Making small changes to your brand, like donning a suit or serving cake on fine china, can have a huge impact.

"85% of your financial success is due to personality and ability to communicate, negotiate, and lead. Shockingly, only 15% is due to technical knowledge."

— CARNEGIE INSTITUTE OF SCIENCE

HOW TO POSITION YOURSELF AS A LUXURY BRAND

We have already established that you are a brand, and that even small changes can raise your perceived value. But what kind of brand are you: high-end, designer, or couture? For maximum impact, you need to market yourself as a luxury brand.

Think of it in terms of watches. An upscale brand watch from Coach or Michael Kors may cost $190-$300. A designer brand watch by Movado will cost you $500-$2000. Cartier, which would be along the lines of a luxury brand, will cost you about $5000-$80,000. Each of these brands has a history and a certain level of craftsmanship that speaks to what you are gaining when you own one of these timepieces.

As a luxury brand, you need to ensure that you are offering your customers something spectacular, as well! Here are some things you can do now to establish yourself as a luxury brand:

BE EXCEPTIONAL.

Offer your clients remarkable customer service. Give them an experience each time they interact with you. Focus on quality and honoring your craft.

TELL YOUR STORY.

Personal branding is emotional. Emotions are contagious. Your story connects the audience to your message, helping you to build relationships.

BE GENUINE.

Be kind, generous, and empathetic.

THE POWER OF PERCEIVED VALUE

BE DIFFERENT.

Focus on what sets you apart.

ELEVATE YOUR PRICE.

People don't value what they don't pay for. Elevated prices help to increase customer focus. They simply pay more attention and are willing to learn what you have to offer.

CAREFULLY CRAFT YOUR IMAGE.

Create a strong brand identity with your website, logo, brand persona, etc.

BE SOCIAL.

You are an expert. Speak, write, and do interviews within your niche.

Luxury brands provide an aura of expertise that is in a league of its own. Marketing yourself as a luxury brand will motivate you to over-deliver. And most importantly, as a luxury brand, you'll attract better customers.

In the next chapter, we'll talk about bringing your image into alignment with the perception you're creating as a luxury brand.

CHAPTER FOUR

THE AMAZING IMPACT OF STYLE

CLOTHING HAS SYMBOLIC MEANING. THE MEANING COMES FROM THE PERSON WEARING THE CLOTHING, AS WELL AS THE IMPRESSION THAT IT INVOKES IN THEIR PSYCHOLOGICAL BLUEPRINT.

The clothing that we wear affects our psychological state and our behavior, causing us to choose clothing that will incite a powerful or hindered task-related performance. This reminds me of the phrase "dress well, test well."

In a study published by Social Psychological & Personality Science, dressing more formally than your peers causes you to think more abstractly, holistically, and creatively.

Hajo Adams and Adam Galinsky from Northwestern University conducted three studies that examined the fact that humans think with both their bodies and their brains. The first test required some participants to wear white lab coats and the other participants to wear street clothes. The purpose of the test was to measure selective attention and their abilities to notice incongruities.

The participants wearing lab coats made half as many mistakes as those wearing street clothes.

In the second study, Adams and Galinsky divided the participants into two groups to test for heightened attention. One group put on doctors' coats; another group put on artistic painters' coats; and the last group was asked to simply look at the doctor's coat that was laid out in front of them as they entered the room. This is interesting because the doctor's coat and the painter's coat were the exact same coat.

The group wearing doctors' coats found more differences than those wearing painters' coats. This displayed heightened attention based on what they perceived the coats to mean while on their bodies.

For the third study, Adams and Galinsky wanted to test whether simply looking at a physical item can affect behavior. They asked some participants to wear the doctors' coats, and the other participants to wear the painters' coats (same coat), while the other participants simply looked at the white lab coat laid in front of them while they took the test.

Each of the participants were asked to write essays about their thoughts on the coats, as well as complete the same visual test of heightened attention. The group that wore the doctors' coats sustained their attention the longest.

These tests show that clothing has symbolic meaning. The meaning comes from the person wearing the clothing, as well as the impression that it invokes in their psychological blueprint.

In other words, people must attribute a symbolic meaning to items in their closet, and wear these items, for the items to have a measurable effect. Think of it as putting on your power each morning.

WHAT'S IN YOUR CLOSET?

Each item in your closet should represent your:

PERSONALITY

THE COLLECTION OF YOUR QUALITIES

CORE VALUES

THE WORTH YOU PUT OUT INTO THE WORLD

THE AMAZING IMPACT OF STYLE

MISSION

AN IMPORTANT GOAL FUELED BY STRONG CONVICTION

VISION

WHAT IS AHEAD

All of this creates the *Image* of your Brand (in other words, looking the part).

IMAGE

YOUR APPEARANCE AND WHAT IT REFLECTS

On the next page, check out what my friends Jesse Garza and Joe Lupo, Creative Directors and co-founders of Visual Therapy, had to say about the power of style during our interview.

INTERVIEW

JESSE GARZA
CO-FOUNDER
AND CREATIVE DIRECTOR
OF **VISUAL THERAPY**

JOE LUPO
CO-FOUNDER
AND CREATIVE DIRECTOR
OF **VISUAL THERAPY**

WHEN YOU PUT TIME AND ENERGY INTO YOUR PERSONAL STYLE, IT REALLY MAKES A BIG DIFFERENCE. IT'S A FORM OF SELF-RESPECT.

FIRST, TELL US ABOUT YOURSELVES!

Joe: Jessie and I started Visual Therapy a long time ago because we love working with people. We really love what we've experienced, not only through ourselves, but through our clients through the years. We love the power of style, how it makes you feel, and how it makes you move through the world.

HOW IMPORTANT IS IMAGE TO YOUR PERSONAL BRAND?

Jessie: We realize that it's not about the clothes, it's about the people. When you wake up in the morning and you open up your wardrobe, you look for the most authentic, almost aspirational version of yourself hanging in your closet. Because when you put that look on, you are branding yourself. When you hit the street, people will judge you. Unfortunately, we live in a world where people do judge. When you walk into a room, they already sum you up.

Joe: Sometimes, the first impression, as you know, is the *only* impression. People hear exactly what they want to hear once they have summed you up. When you wake up in the morning, especially if you wake up on the wrong side of the bed, that's the day where you need to put extra effort into the way you look. If you go out the door, feeling the best that you can possibly be dressed, it'll completely affect the way you are perceived and received for the rest of the day. How you choose to dress will determine whether your day is going to go really well, or whether it's going to go down the toilet. We've all had days where we don't bother with dressing well and then our day just keeps going down.

HOW IMPORTANT IS IT TO FIND YOUR SIGNATURE PERSONAL STYLE?

Jessie: It's so important—it changes everything. Most women, for example, are caregivers. They put a lot of energy into taking care of everyone around them, but not themselves. When you put time and energy into your personal style, it really makes a big difference. It's a form of self-respect.

Joe: It is a form of self-respect; you have to think of yourself as a brand. We've even ventured into home visual therapy now because we understand how important it is not only that you look great but that your surroundings represent who you are. You see, if you put on some outfit and it doesn't feel like it's *you*, there's going to be a disconnect, and you're not going to move through the day feeling like the best version of yourself. Whereas if you can really start to understand your style, you'll show up as your best self. One way to understand your style is to get inspired by looking at things and people that you admire. If there's an influencer that you admire, you can begin to emulate their style. Keep taking steps towards finding your own personal style and once you do that, you will become unstoppable.

Jessie: At Visual Therapy, we strongly believe in having a zen closet. When you open up your closet doors, you need to experience peaceful and empowered feelings. When we work with our private clients we organize their closets, arranging it so they can dress well. Not everyone has the style gene, and that is okay. There are formulas and things that you can teach yourself. There are ways to be inspired, so that you know what speaks to you, and you can define your style. When you get dressed and go out into the world, it's not just you, it's the best version of you.

WHAT'S YOUR ADVICE FOR DRESSING WELL?

Joe: We teach our clients that you need to be pro-active when you choose your look for the day. You can't be reactive. You have to invest a little bit of time and energy into your look. For example, when it's Sunday night, take 10-20 minutes go through your closet and pull together looks for the week. Choose what you'll wear on Monday and plan a look for your upcoming event.

Jessie: Choose the category—date night, business, a lunch—as though you're putting together a lineup of a fashion show.

Joe: A line-up of your greatest hits.

Jessie: Everything should be greatest hits.

Joe: Yeah.

Jessie: And it's also about having fun. At the end of day, style and fashion should not be a pain. It should be a way to celebrate.

Joe: Dressing well is like the frosting on the cake. You're the cake—what's beautiful and amazing is *you*—and what you put on yourself is going to help you put your image out there. Dressing well helps you let the world know what you're trying to portray. By lining up your looks, like Jesse said earlier, you're prepared to add the sweetness every time you get dressed. Each day when you're getting ready and you're running around in the morning, you can grab something to put it on, knowing that this is already a thought out, put together look, instead of just grabbing something and running out the door. Whichever way you get dressed in the morning is the same way the rest of your day is going to go.

Jessie: What's also important is understanding who you are working for. What is their brand? What do they represent? Because when you go to work, you're not only representing yourself as a brand, you're representing your employer, or a corporate brand. It's okay to self-express with your look, but let's say you're *not* within the parameters of the dress code. Maybe in your heart, you're a whimsical girl, and you like bells and whistles and polka dots and florals and whatever…

Joe: But you're going to work at a bank, right?

Jessie: Right. So maybe wear a fun print in your blouse and not in your entire outfit. You can express yourself fully on the weekends. But at work, keep in mind that you're representing another brand.

Joe: That's such an important point, because if you blow that, you might just blow that next career move for yourself. You might think it's only going to affect the way other coworkers react to you, but there's more on the line. Once again, you are your own brand. You have to identify your brand and stick to it.

Jessie: I have a story. Joe, do you remember our client when we first started our business? She came to us and said, "I don't know what it is. I'm an attorney. I just made a partner. But every time I walk into a conference room, people ask me for coffee."

Joe: She was a little bit of a bohemian, brilliant girl who graduated from Harvard. Really amazing.

Jessie: And she had great energy.

Joe: Everything changed for her after evolving her wardrobe. After working with us and putting a new look together while giving her a style where she felt like herself, she felt powerful. And when we say powerful, it's not dressing like a man or wearing some weird suit...

Jessie: You need to embrace who you are. Our client was a woman, for example. I think a lot of women think they have to look like a man to get what they need, but I disagree. I think you can really embrace your femininity and put on a dress. You can wear a feminine look that emits the same power as a suit.

Jessie: Our client got the formulas down. She lined up looks that represented the best version of herself. We empowered her to knock it up a notch to make her personal style aspirational. When she came back to us, she shared an amazing testimonial.

Joe: She said, "I walked into the conference room. And because of the way I looked, my job was already halfdone. I walked in and I immediately commanded the attention that I should have commanded as a woman in my position". For our client, everything just changed. It changed everything.

WHAT'S YOUR ADVICE TO MEN?

Joe: Dressing well does the same thing for our male clients—until they go out on the weekends, wearing shoddy clothing. This man may run a huge corporation but he's wearing something that is so distasteful in his casual life.

Jessie: Men can throw on a suit—it's like a uniform. But on the weekend, they're pulling out some old college sweatshirt and they look lazy or crazy or both. Men definitely benefit from having a stylist, to have someone categorize and line up their looks.

Joe: Once they have a formula, they are good to go, because it's a formulaic approach to everything. The biggest mistake that men make is thinking that they don't have to put any effort into it. A lot of times men say, "You know, I'm smart, I don't have to do that, I don't need to do that." There are two significant problems when you think that you don't need to do dress well — A. you're dismissing people, and B. people are going to judge you the second you see them. And a lot of times you'll see someone come in, out in the Hamptons, the richest guy will wear a t-shirt and flip flops to a party. Even though it is definitely not a t-shirt and flip flop party, he knows he's the richest guy in the room. What does that say to people?

Jessie: I don't care.

Joe: What he's basically saying is, "I don't respect you all enough to give you the best version of who I am."

If you're the leader of a company, people are looking up to you, they admire you. You need to set an example. If you're not setting an example, then you're basically saying that the brand of your company isn't important enough to represent in a good way.

ARE THERE ANY FINAL THOUGHTS THAT YOU'D LIKE TO SHARE?

Joe: Another thing that we talked about in our book, *Work It*, was being appropriate. Like dressing age-appropriate, or dressing appropriate for the workplace, or being appropriate for the date night, for example. When you're thinking about yourself as a brand, you have to also think about the signals that you're putting out there. If you're wondering why you're not being taken seriously, then maybe you need to take a look at what you're wearing.

Jessie: We have a client who's mega high powered, and she sat me down in her office once, and she said,

"I just want to tell you how grateful I am for what you do for us because every time I start my day, I feel so organized and put together. I know that when I walk out that door, I can focus on my job, zero in on my gifts and knock it out of the park instead of thinking about how my shoes hurt or worrying whether my outfit is crazy." There's so much going on in the world and the last thing that should hold you back is your outfit.

"Fashion says, 'Me, too;' a powerful brand image says, 'Only me.'"

— - TOI SWEENEY

OUTFIT VS. LOOK

Okay, let's address some of the language that you heard in the video.

What's the difference between fashion and style?

- **Fashion is what you buy**
- **Style is how you put it together**

What the difference between and outfit and a look? Dictionary.com describes an outfit as "a set of clothes worn together for a particular occasion and purpose." Each season, brick-and-mortar stores put together catalogues with beautiful outfits. These lifestyle shots sell you the story.

Each season's designers put together "look books." When you put together a "look," you're expressing a specific brand message. Looks are not typically shot in lifestyle settings. Looks send the message that it does not matter where you're going, your goal is to conquer the day! Looks have stopping power.

SECRETS OF A WELL DRESSED BRAND

01. OUTFIT

01. LOOK

01. OUTFIT

01. LOOK

THE AMAZING IMPACT OF STYLE

03. OUTFIT

03. LOOK

PORTRAITS OF EXCEPTIONAL STYLE

1) CORY NIEVES

You are never too young to have achieved exceptional style. One of my favorite CEOs that has exceptional style is the once 13-year-old Cory Nieves of Mr. Cory's Cookies. You may have seen Cory's story five years ago on the Ellen DeGeneres show. If you haven't, it's worth the time.

Mr. Cory's understands the importance of building a personal brand identity. It's important to project the right brand image if he wants to sell cookies.

It's impossible to meet Mr. Cory and not love him. He is kind and humble, super stylish, and sweet. His delicious cookies reflect his personal brand. Mr. Cory is well-known on the who's who list of fashion movers and shakers, and is loved among foodies! He is a well-dressed brand.

2) GARY VAYNERCHUK, DAVE RAMSEY, & SETH GODIN

I had the pleasure of seeing Gary Vaynerchuk (or Gary Vee), Dave Ramsey, and Seth Godin speak a few years ago. I couldn't help but notice what each of the men decided to wear for the event.

Gary Vee was wearing skinny jeans, a sweater, and pink high-top sneakers. Gary Vee is the epitome of personal branding. I love that his style speaks to being true to who you are, period. (And a few F-bombs later, it was quite clear that he is unapologetically himself). His personal band is about not being fancy. It's all about working incredibly hard so that it's impossible for people to not notice who you are!

Dave Ramsey was wearing a sport coat, dark denim straight-leg jeans, a plaid shirt, brown shoes, and a brown belt. Very approachable and professional, which is what I would expect from

Dave. Dave displays a consistent brand, both online and in person.

Seth Godin was wearing a very well-tailored gray suit, paired with a light-colored shirt and a pocket square. I noticed that, toward the end of the seminar, Seth changed into dark jeans and a nice shirt. The casual look was approachable, yet fashionable.

All three men dressed according to their personal brands.

3) JANELLE MONÁE

When I think of someone else who used their image to propel them forward, I think of singer-songwriter Janelle Monáe. Ms. Monáe has a few Grammys under her belt, and may be best known for her role in the movie *Hidden Figures*.

It's obvious that Janelle Monáe is very talented. The reason she sticks out to me as having an iconic personal brand is because being a beautiful girl dropping an album is a bit of a commodity in the music industry.

I first discovered Janelle while perusing Vogue magazine one day. Her exceptional style landed her a prestigious spread. As I began to do some research, I realize that she was famous for keeping her clothes on, which demanded that you see her true beauty and undeniable talent. Her style is individual and personal. She is amazing!

Now that she has established her brand, I've begun noticing that she is showing a little more skin. However, it's still not over-the-top sexy; it's just simple and beautiful. Sex sells; instead of leaking a sex tape, she did not wait for an opportunity to knock—she built a door instead! And on the other side of that door stood a queen that kept her clothes on.

HOW DO I STYLE MYSELF IF I'M EMPLOYED BY A BRAND?

What if you are not the CEO or in the entertainment industry? When you are employed by someone else, you have to be able to artfully mesh your personal brand with the brand of the company. Simply put, follow the dress code, consider your audience each day, and add elements of your signature style to stand out for the right reasons.

And, there's good news! Companies today realize the importance of employees having strong personal brands. It adds to the value of the company. We love people and connections, not corporations. For example, when you listen to a podcast, you're tuning in to hear the host, right?

Companies can be sold, people get new jobs—but your personal brand will live on, regardless of what you do for a living.

DO YOU KNOW HOW TO DETERMINE YOUR STYLE?

Knowing how to determine your style is one of the most powerful tools you will ever use. Style breaks down into six categories: *Innovative, Powerful, Ladylike, Timeless, Effortless, and Polished.*

You probably already have an idea what your personal style is all about, but take the style quiz near the back of this book on page 165 so that you are 100% sure.

Check the results against the items in your closet. This will help you see where you have been making purchasing mistakes, plus help you understand which type of items you gravitate toward in a store, and why.

In the next chapter, I'll help you use what you've learned about your personal style to help you start becoming a well-dressed brand.

CHECKLIST

Make sure your closet is set up for you to succeed.

- [ ] Remove any items in your closet that do not send the proper message for work create sections for date night, work out, zoom meetings, etc.

- [ ] Make sure that you have items that fit you. Make sure the items are not too tight or too revealing, or too loose.

- [ ] Find a good tailor and a good shoe repair place. Make sure you have good grooming habits: Fresh haircut, clean nail, a good skin care, and hygiene routine.

- [ ] Make sure clothing is not wrinkled, shoes are free from scuff marks, and no visual stains on clothing.

CHAPTER FIVE

HOW TO BECOME

A WELL DRESSED BRAND

YOU NEED A SIGNATURE STYLE TO CRAFT YOUR UNIQUE PACKAGING. REMOVE ANY ITEMS IN YOUR CLOSET THAT DO NOT SEND THE PROPER MESSAGE.

The first step toward becoming a well-dressed brand is creating your brand mantra, or anthem (as in *Sally Hogshead's Fascination Advantage®* assessment). This is different from your mission statement. Your mission statement is about *you*. Your branding statement is about the customer.

In personal branding, your brand mantra is about what you deliver to everyone else that sets you apart.

Let's take a quick look at Nike, a great example of branding for product. Nike's mission statement is, "Bringing inspiration and innovation to every athlete in the world." But Nike's brand mantra is, "Just Do It." Want to crush that Iron Man this weekend? "Just Do It."

My personal branding mission statement is, "Guiding you to exceptional style." But my anthem is, "Shut-It-Down Style." In other words, doing one thing the best and hardest that it can be done. (For example, you walk into a meeting with a client and your style "shuts it down.")

To begin this process, I suggest that you take the Fascination Advantage® test. Your personality, or the beautiful collection of your qualities, is what makes you fascinating. Are you able to brilliantly communicate the brand message that you are already sending out without trying?

This assessment is different than *Myers-Briggs* and the *Gallup StrengthsFinder*. Those tests focus on how you see the world. In contrast, the Fascination Advantage® shows you how the world sees you. You can't imagine what a weight will come off your shoulders when you learn what people are saying about you when you're not in the room.

This test provides you with five adjectives that describe how you add value, how you lead, and how you work well on teams. You will also get one-minute coaching and a chance to create your brand anthem!

Below is a snapshot of my test and picture of what you can expect to receive. The results of your assessment can help you become a well-dressed brand.

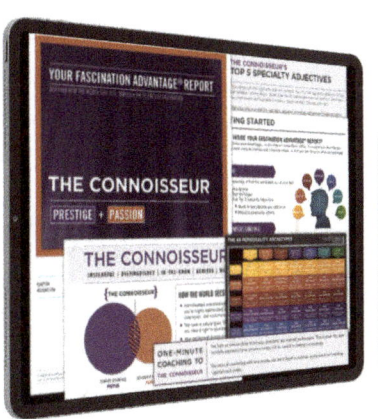

©*How to Fascinate* and Sally Hogshead. All rights reserved. Used with Permission.

SECRETS OF A WELL DRESSED BRAND

TAKE THE FASCINATION ADVANTAGE® TEST

Or type https://ea106.isrefer.com/go/CFFAA/TOISWEENEY/ into your browser.

HOW TO USE COLOR TO DRESS MEANINGFULLY

The second step to becoming a well-dressed brand is using and understanding the psychology behind each color.

According to Yellow Duck Marketing, here is

why the power of color is so awesome:

- **92.2 % of consumers report that visual factors are the most important when buying a product**
- **62%-90% of people initially judge a product based solely on color** (Source: Yellow Duck Marketing)

Think back to the first time you saw the all-white Apple products—specifically, the white headphones or the white box! White was different; it stood out in a sea of black headphones. The psychological meaning behind the color white is "new beginnings." The color suggests, "Why not start over with a clean slate—a blank canvas just waiting to be written on?" "Think Different" is their brand anthem.

What about the color red, used by Target and Pinterest? The psychological meaning of the color red is passion—strong, spontaneous, and confident. Target suggests that you "Expect More."

As you can see, color is a great way to drive your

message home. From the colors of your logo to the colors used on your website, color matters! Are the colors in your closet indicative of the brand message you want to send? Remove any items in your closet that do not send the proper message.

THE PSYCHOLOGY OF COLOR

WHITE

The color of newness, hope, simplicity, and equality. White tells the world you're fair, simple, self-sufficient, and whole.

GRAY

The color of elegance, stability, and dependability. Gray tells the world you're solid, classic, and stable.

BROWN

The color of quiet, strength, honesty, and reliability. Brown tells the world you're loyal and trustworthy.

BLACK

The color of authority, power, determination, and confidence. Black tells the world you're independent and sophisticated.

BLUE

The color of trust, perseverance, caring, integrity, responsibility, and authority. Blue tells the world you're idealistic, orderly, and a peacemaker.

INDIGO

The color of selflessness, structure, and sincerity. Indigo tells the world you're highly intuitive, creative, and visionary.

PURPLE

The color of compassion, wealth, luxury, and spirituality. Purple tells the world you're regal, set apart, and you demand respect.

PINK

The color of connection, understanding, love, and empathy. Pink tells the world you're intuitive, innocent, and hopeful.

RED

The color of ambition, determination, assertiveness, confidence, and power. Red tells the world you're courageous, driven, and you take action.

ORANGE

The color of adventure, creativity, and forward-thinking. Orange tells the world you're enthusiastic, a risk-taker, informal, and extroverted.

YELLOW

The color of originality, intellect, happiness, and fun. Yellow tells the world you're wise, confident, and optimistic.

GREEN

The color of growth, kindness, loyalty, and compassion. Green tells the world you're dependable, generous, self-reliant, and calm.

TURQUOISE

The color of communication, clarity, and idealism. Turquoise tells the world you're creative, clear-headed, and self-sufficient.

Start with your basic colors, like black, navy, tan, and ivory; make sure these colors are covered. You can match almost any color to these basics, or wear these colors monochromatically to create a long, lean, elegant look (women).

Wearing black, gray, navy or ivory is very elegant. Add pops of color with your lipsticks and shoes. So if you're wearing all gray, you can wear pink lipstick and pink pumps.

Here are some other color suggestions for women:

- Make sure your shoes match the colors of your tops
- Choose a basic A-line or pencil skirt in black, navy, tan, or ivory
- When it comes to jeans, you can't miss with black, dark indigo, gray, and white jeans

And for the men:

- Choose three colors of slacks and sport coats:

black, navy, gray, brown, or tan
- You can't go wrong with black, gray, or dark denim jeans
- Always have white and blue button-collar and spread-collar shirts on hand
- Make sure you have shoes and socks that match your pants (for example, gray pants with gray socks, unless you're wearing brown shoes—then you can wear brown socks)

GIVE YOUR LOOK A TWIST WITH A SIGNATURE STYLE

You are well on your way to becoming a well-dressed brand. How will your clothing (your packaging) be unique to you?

You need a signature style to craft your unique packaging. When you think of great fashion icons, a picture pops into your mind, right? What you're thinking of is their signature look.

Here are some tips for creating your own signature look:

- First, start with something very personal to you or an interest that you have. It can be anything: a piece of jewelry with your children or pets' names on it, playing golf, shopping, horses, etc.

- Glasses are a great way to create a signature look. If you have to wear them anyway, you might as well be known for having cool ones! Make sure you have a few pairs that you can switch between looks (tortoise, navy, clear, red, etc.).

- Color is a great way to stand out. I think of Steve Jobs and his black turtleneck, or Tabatha Coffey and her all-black everything.

- Try different color palettes, like olive green and

blush, or taupe and white, or army green and fuchsia. Gray and navy always look good on male and females.

— Shoes, unique scarves, and handbags are always a great way to create a signature look.

— Adding pops of color on your nails and lips is another great way to go.

— If choosing something more classic for you signature items, like a classic white shirt, make sure the item has a bit of a twist on the design: maybe a white button-down with a stripe pocket, etc.

— Men, grab a great pair of fashionable sneakers, remove the traditional laces, and replace them with a unique shoelace that speaks to your personal brand.

These are just a few very general ideas that you can try. Have fun with it!

In the next chapter, we'll talk about how to create a brand-right closet, and I'll give you a sneak peek of this style strategy in action.

GREAT IDEAS FOR CREATING YOUR SIGNATURE STYLE

REMINDERS:
Play with color and texture. Invest in your accessories.
Let your personality show!

COURAGEOUS | CONFIDENT | POWERFUL

THE PSYCHOLOGY OF COLOR

INTEGRITY | AUTHORITY

ORIGINAL | OPTIMISTIC

FAIR | SELF-SUFFICIENT

GENEROUS | SELF-RELIANT

THE PSYCHOLOGY OF COLOR   THE PSYCHOLOGY OF COLOR   THE PSYCHOLOGY OF COLOR

CLASSIC | DEPENDABLE

INTUITIVE | HOPEFUL

CHAPTER SIX

HOW TO CREATE A BRAND-RIGHT CLOSET

IT'S IMPORTANT TO REFRAME YOUR THINKING SO THAT YOU LOOK AND FEEL YOUR BEST. WHEN YOU LOOK AND FEEL YOUR BEST, YOU DEMAND THAT THE WORLD SEES YOU THE SAME WAY.

Creating and maintaining a brand-right closet will help you to cut down on making the wrong choices. The purpose of creating a brand-right closet is to the take the hassle out of what to wear each day. Everything in your closet will speak to your personal brand, creating a great sense of personal style.

Women have more options than men, which makes it harder to simplify—not to mention, we have to carry a change of shoes and dress in layers, depending on what we need to tackle on any given day. All of this can be a challenge if you are unaware of what your style is altogether (refer to the quiz on page 165 if you haven't already!).

To create a brand-right closet, we are going to build a capsule wardrobe. The phrase "capsule wardrobe" was coined by Suzi Fox, a boutique owner in London. Fox was ahead of her time; she loved the concept of dressing in a small collection of clothing each season.

The key component of capsule dressing is only allowing yourself a certain number of items each season, depending on the size of your closet. Each item fits within a certain color palette that can be mixed and matched.

Start by completely emptying out your closet. Remove anything that does not speak to your personal brand and the message that you want to send out to the world. Are the items adding to your perceived value, or are they just taking up space?

Create four piles, keeping a few items that you wear to work around the house:

1. The Yes Pile: Yes, this item is brand-right! ("I feel authentically myself.")

2. The No Pile: No, this is not brand-right. ("Not sure why I bought this—donate!")

3. Items separated by season.

4. Work items separated from weekend wear.

This is just a quick snapshot into creating a capsule wardrobe. To take a deeper dive, check out the blog *un-fancy*.

Now that you're ready to shop, here is a quick

guide to elevating your look even more:

- **Have a good tailor.** This is especially important for men. Fit is key to making a great first impression. For women, clothing today is not the same as it was years ago. It's very difficult to purchase things off the rack that are perfect. You may have to get the waist taken in or hem your jeans to ensure that things are hitting you in the correct places. Thankfully, most department stores have an in-house seamstress.
- **Invest in your accessories:** shoes, bags, ties, watches, cufflinks, scarves, handbags, etc.
- **Have a good shoe repair place.** You may not need to buy new shoes each season, especially if you're buying quality. You may need to replace the sole or the heel, or have your shoes polished, which is a lot more cost-effective than buying a new pair.
- **Be a good steward of your wardrobe;** make

sure your closet is stocked with lint rollers, stain sticks, double-sided fashion tape, safety pins, etc.

- **Make sure all of your clothing is pressed.** This makes a huge difference in your appearance. Most people hate to iron, so they purchase wrinkle-free shirts and pants. Because most people just toss their clothing on in the morning, this small change will really make you stand out.
- **Practice great grooming habits** (like fresh haircuts, clean nails, and well-groomed beards for men). Most women keep steady manicure and pedicure appointments.
- **Make sure you have a great skincare routine**, whether you wear makeup or not.
- **Drink plenty of water.**

You are a luxury brand! You can make small changes to your brand to elevate it, giving you a very expensive look.

This is not about being perfect. But it's important to reframe your thinking so that you look and feel your best. When you look and feel your best, you demand that the world sees you the same way.

THE CAPSULE WARDROBE IN ACTION

The alarm goes off at 7:50 a.m. *Son of a biscuit eater!* I have ten minutes before I need to leave for work. Ten minutes to get my son off to summer camp.

I run down the hall and slap on his camp shirt and a pair of shorts, hustle him into the kitchen, and slide him a bowl of cereal.

As I run upstairs to get dressed, I remember that I have a 10 a.m. meeting!

I burst into my closet and grab a black pencil

skirt with a side slit and a black V-neck t-shirt off the floor. Next, I shove my leopard print wedges and matching scarf into my handbag, slip on my nude flip-flops, and head out the door.

I speed into the work parking lot around 9:40 a.m., run into the ladies' room, and attempt to not look dead by smearing makeup all over my face. I apply a red lip stain, tie on the scarf, and slip on my wedges. I only stop by my desk long enough to grab a notepad and pen, then off I go.

On the way down the hall, I can't believe how many compliments I get on my outfit. I keep thinking to myself, *"Are these people nuts?"*

After my meeting, my co-worker stops me and says, "You always know how to put things together!"

"Yeah, this was on my closet floor this morning," I say.

"Really? You have an eye."

I smile. "Honestly, I have finally gotten my closet to the point that everything works, no matter what."

As I drive the hour home that night, I have to admit that for getting dressed in less than ten minutes, I did pretty well.

Why? Because I buy basic apparel items and trend-right accessories. I match my accessories, but I may not always wear them together. For example, I own a navy silk shirt dress and a navy fur vest that I wear with navy tights and navy booties during the winter months. (Monochromatic colors make you look longer and leaner.)

During the spring and summer months, I wear the same dress with bare legs and navy wedge sandals or nude strappy sandals. I carry a forest green handbag in the winter months and tan handbag in the summer.

Nearly everything in my closet is transitional. I can take it from season to season without too much of a hassle. Since winter months are longer, I spend more money on fall clothing.

I own one to two pairs of designer sandals.

Typically, I do not spend a lot of money on sandals unless I can wear them most of the year, or if they were a tremendous value.

It's important to access your lifestyle and make your closet work for you. Create a brand-right closet space that reflects your inner beauty and your brand—a zen space, as Jess and Joe discussed in Chapter Four.

In the next chapter, I'll walk you through the roles of image consultants and fashion stylists—then help you decide whether you need to hire one to help you craft your brand-right style.

CHAPTER SEVEN

DO YOU NEED

AN IMAGE CONSULTANT OR FASHION STYLIST?

IT IS IMPORTANT FOR YOU TO HAVE A STRONG VISUAL IDENTITY ACROSS THE BOARD. YOU ARE YOUR BRAND'S PERSONA AND THE FACE OF YOUR BRAND.

The purpose of your image is to maximize the impact of your nonverbal communications. Your image should reflect the likeness of personal brand; it includes all of your visual marketing collateral, from your logo to your social media profiles, and even includes what you choose to wear.

It is important for you to have a strong visual identity across the board. You are your brand's persona and the face of your brand.

How do you know if you need help with your image? I'm not going to tell you to ask your friends, because they love you and will not tell you the truth. So, instead…think about your wardrobe for a second.

When was the last time you updated your look? What about your clothing? Have you been wearing

"You are your brand's persona and the face of your brand."

— - TOI SWEENEY

the same style and cut for the last 5 years, or are you making small updates each season to stay relevant?

I don't want you to settle for just looking "fine," or "OK." Why would you settle for that? You should be remarkable, stunning, magnificent, and gorgeous.

If you are not blessed with having a great eye for style, then it's time to hire a fashion stylist or image consultant. What's the difference?

Although there is some crossover between the two jobs, here it is:

- Image consultants know the "why" behind style; they've memorized the rulebook!
- Fashion stylists know the "how" and tend to work on instinct; they just know what looks good.

Image consultants, typically, will do closet edits and closet clean-outs. They will perform a color analysis, educating you on things like the colors you should wear and your body type. You may hear them use terms like, "You are winter," or "summer," or "clear," to describe the color of your hair, eyes, and complexion.

They will educate you on where articles of clothing and accessories should fall on your body. They often use a point system to help you learn how to accessorize.

Image consultants tend to work for corporations that help them to define the code. Some image consultants also offer media training, in which they help you to speak competently on camera.

Fashion stylists typically work for magazines, television stations, and other media companies, creating looks using accessories, clothing, and other props to create visually stunning style stories. They create fashion-forward looks that are trend-driven.

Fashion stylists tend to work with fashion models as they learn to master the art of pinning the wardrobe to perfection to create the desired outcome. In other words, fashion stylists create "looks," not outfits.

The celebrity stylist builds great relationships with designer and couture houses to get their clients ready for the red carpet and other events. Celebrity stylists also influence hair and makeup at times. Not all fashion stylists can put together everyday looks, and not all image consultants can make you look relevant and on-trend.

Make sure that you do your homework on the image consultant or fashion stylist you choose. This is a very important relationship, as you are inviting someone into your home (it's not uncommon for a fashion stylist or image consultant to have a key to his or her client's house). Most stylist and image consultants work virtually today.

Often, busy clients like you may need outfits or looks put together in a certain time frame. The purpose of stylists and consultants is to ensure that you look the part, save time, and can focus on doing your job, as opposed to worrying about how you look.

When it comes to choosing between hiring an

image consultant or a fashion stylist, I don't think that one choice is better than the other. You just have to choose someone who will work well with your personality and who will deliver what you need. Remember, what we do is not unique; the value comes from the person.

I consider myself a brand image stylist. With both a fashion styling and image consulting background, I am also a certified branding coach. I help my clients create signature looks, build their personal brands, and lead with exceptional personal style. I love that today, I get to work with clients all over the country because we can work via FaceTime or Skype.

I had the pleasure of hearing Ann Ewers, CEO of the Kimmel Center in Philadelphia, give a keynote a while back. Anne told a story about how her mentor suggested that she take charge of her image. Check out what she had to say.

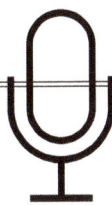

INTERVIEW

ANN EWERS
PRESIDENT & CEO OF **KIMMEL CULTURAL CAMPUS**

"NO MATTER HOW MUCH YOU CHANGE ON THE OUTSIDE, YOU WON'T HAVE ANYTHING TO OFFER IF YOU DON'T CHANGE ON THE INSIDE." - ANN EWERS

YOU HAVE A UNIQUE AND POWERFUL MAKEOVER STORY. CAN YOU TELL US ABOUT IT?

When someone runs a nonprofit arts organization or a nonprofit organization, the minute somebody says, "We have a fundraising opportunity for you, you just grab it."

So, when this spa in Salt Lake said, "Look, we're opening a spa; we want to get a CEO guinea pig to promote what we do," I was on it.

If it's a fundraising opportunity, I thought, let's go for it. Timing is always very important.

At that same time, I was working with a mentor and working on some internal transformations of myself. And so, it all just kind of happened as it should.

The idea was that I would have this makeover and that they would then use that as an opportunity to promote the spa. So, we started with this wonderful gal who came to my house. She came with these big bins and a couple of collapsible hanging racks.

We went through my entire closet, and she would pick up something, and she would say, "How old is this?" And I would say, "Oh, 15 years or whatever, thank you for your service." And she would dump it into the bin.

We ended up spending half a day throwing out

over half of my clothing. After she left, I was so excited by this process that I threw out another third. I mean, I was just on it.

Then we went shopping. It was fascinating finding out what was best for my body shape, and what was best alignment, in terms of lengths of things. I frankly had curly frizzy hair and thick glasses. I had a box suit, and my dresses went down to mid-calf. It's really sad when you see the before pictures, but the after pictures are really pretty stunning.

After we did all that, she said, "Okay, now we need to do the hair."

Well, I panicked. I thought, "Oh my God, what am I? I've had the same hairstyle for forever."

So we went to a stylist; we did the whole thing. But the final piece was the glasses. I had worn contacts for 25 years, but it was just too dry in Salt Lake and I couldn't wear them anymore. Now I was wearing these thick glasses. So, they came up with a solution. I got implantable contact lenses during a three-hour surgery. When I woke up after the surgery, I could see. It was really a transformation.

The most important part of that transformation was that yes, I'd physically changed on the outside, but if I hadn't been changing on the inside, none of the outside changes would have mattered.

WHAT LESSONS HAVE YOU LEARNED?

One of the lessons I learned was to listen. My mentor said, "I've never seen anybody work a room like you do." And then he said, "Have you ever thought about listening more and talking less? Try, at the next reception you're doing, to listen to what the people are saying and say very little about yourself. Leave that night having said very little."

Well, it was fascinating because I learned much more by listening. And interestingly enough, other people began to talk about the organization. How much better to have others touting the organization, than me touting the organization. Listening became a marvelous tool and something that I've continued doing.

Another lesson I learned was: when getting dressed always consider your audience. Who are you meeting? Who are you talking to? Not that you're going to change your whole style accordingly, but what do you have in your closet that can make whoever you're meeting with feel comfortable, feel at ease, and feel a connection?

YOU'VE MENTIONED HOW YOU CHANGED ON THE INSIDE. HOW SIGNIFICANT IS INTERNAL GROWTH?

No matter how much you change on the outside, you won't have anything to offer if you don't change on the inside.

We all need to thoroughly and fully understand ourselves and accept ourselves. A person can tell when the confidence isn't there. When the sense of love of self, when the embrace of self is missing, it's obvious. People have to understand that they need to know themselves and understand themselves, and then let that embrace of themselves reflect outward.

IS THERE ONE THING YOU'VE NOTICED REGARDING HOW PEOPLE DRESS FOR WORK THAT DRIVES YOU CRAZY?

The thing that drives me crazy is what people do about shoes. Someone may look spectacular, and then you look at their feet...

Folks don't realize that if you spend the money and buy a couple of quality pairs of shoes, you'll be set up for success instead of having a lot of different shoes that wear out in less than a season. Second to that is to find a good shoe repair service.

There's nothing worse than hearing a clack-clack sound coming down the hall. You can hear the clacking sound because either the front or back of a shoe has worn down or, even worse — the shoe's heel has begun to roll up.

The top topic in my conversations with my mentees is "shoes." Shoes set people apart. You can tell who is completely dressed, top to bottom, by what they have on their feet and the condition of their shoes. It's a simple thing that people need to be aware of: watch the shoes. People generally make "shoe contact" before "eye contact".

"Dress for the job you want, not for the job you have."

— - TOI SWEENEY

Does this still hold true today? Yes—it happened to me! (Remember my story about deliberately changing my image to fit the promotion I wanted?)

The CEO and other leaders in any company set the tone for how other employees should dress. Even if your coworkers decide to be more casual or dressy, depending on the company, that has nothing to do with you. Consider your goals, your mission, and your vision.

I hope this interview with Ann gets you thinking about your image and how you can elevate your brand. Remember, your brand image reaches your customers before your talent and personality even have a chance to shine.

CHAPTER EIGHT

PUTTING IT ALL TOGETHER

ARE YOU READY TO LOOK, FEEL, AND CONFIDENTLY OFFER YOUR TRUE SELF TO THE WORLD?

Let's look at the outcome when you put all these principles into practice.

I'd like to introduce you to Andrea Weinberg, author of *Unfrozen: Stop Holding Back and Release the Real You*. Andrea is also host of the *Voice of Influence* podcast.

Like a lot of women, Andrea is a very successful entrepreneur. When it came to her personal brand, she wanted to make sure that her voice and brand message were being heard. When Andrea first reached out to me, she shared what she felt was holding her back from being a well-dressed brand.

FROM ANDREA:

"I was never too interested in how I looked as a kid. It was really important to me that people valued me for who I was on the inside, not how I looked on the outside. In fact, I clung so tightly to that aspiration that I refused to wear the 'cool' jeans or shop at the stores with more expensive clothes. My general attitude was, "Take me to the clearance racks and I'll find something that's comfortable!

"But as I approach 40 and kick my career into high gear after a few years at home with our kids, I have a different perspective. Who I am on the inside is great and all, but if I can't express that on the outside, I'm not going to be able to make the difference I want to make in the world. I know I have what it takes to write, speak, and inspire others to find and develop their own voice of influence, but I definitely don't show that in my fashion style right now. It's time to transition from 'casual mom who just wants to be comfortable' to 'professional woman, ready to stand up and make the impact I'm called to make.'

PUTTING IT ALL TOGETHER

"The problem is, I have no idea what I'm doing! That's why I need to hire you. I appreciate that you are taking time to understand who I am on the inside so you can help me express that on the outside. According to the Fascination Advantage®, I'm The Maverick Leader (Innovation + Power). After years of holding back, I'm finally ready to own this expression of my personality. But I need help conveying that through my style."

"I've wasted lots of time, energy and money on clothing that just doesn't quite work. Honestly, I don't have time to waste anymore. It's important to me that I invest in a wardrobe that will not only express my identity, but will last beyond a single season. It's time to be me, inside and out. I'm so thankful I found you!"

—ANDREA WEINBERG

During our personal branding consultation, I asked Andrea to take the style test. The test revealed that her style needs to be effortless but polished, and that we would be shopping for pretty classic items.

As Andrea is booked for conferences and promoting her book and podcast, it's very important that she looks like the leader and expert that she is.

SECRETS OF A WELL DRESSED BRAND

Here's a glimpse into our interaction:

> **TOI:** "What do you want people to say about you when you're not in the room?"
>
> **ANDREA:** "She's approachable and insightful. I need to listen to her, and maybe she'll even help me solve some of my problems."
>
> **TOI:** "What colors do you hate?"
>
> **ANDREA:** "I am not sure. I tend to lean toward dark and light blue, white, and otherwise neutral colors. I probably just don't like really super-bright colors."

I began working on a customer color analysis branding roadmap so that after we shop, Andrea can maintain dressing to her full potential.

Here is a snapshot of Andrea's customized branding report:

©How to Fascinate and Sally Hogshead. All rights reserved. Used with Permission.

The Fascination Advantage® report revealed that she is The Maverick Leader, which means she naturally leads with innovation and power. Maverick leaders lead with a bold, unconventional vision; they are independent and confident.

The style personality test, along with the Fascination Advantage® test, provided us with a great blueprint to ensure Andrea will project a strong brand image. As you can see from both tests, Andrea is already everything that she wants and needs to be. It's just a matter of looking the part. Here's what Andrea had to say about the experience:

> "When I walked into the dressing room full of clothing and shoes Toi picked out for me to try, my whole being opened up.
>
> "It was evident to me that I could trust my appearance to her care because she took the time to understand who I was, what I was comfortable with, and how much I was willing to be stretched. And sure enough, the very first shirt she had me try on fit who I am perfectly and totally transformed the way I thought about myself."

BEFORE:

AFTER:

HAIR AND MAKE-UP BY LIA KEY

PUTTING IT ALL TOGETHER

'Wow! I really do look like I have something important to say!' That was exactly what I hoped to portray with my new look.

"Toi showed me the visual tricks to use for my body type that would help me look taller and made suggestions about how to mix and match the items we chose for various kinds of occasions."

"One unexpected benefit from the experience was learning how the clothes I previously wore made me appear older than I am. It was breathtaking to see years fall off with my new style!"

"After a few hours trying on clothes and seeing Toi work her magic adjusting sleeves, belts, and collars, I made my final purchasing decisions and walked out with the confidence of knowing that I would now be a well-dressed brand."

"As soon as I got home, I cleaned out most of my closet and chose to keep a few items that would fit with the colors and style Toi created for me. Now I am ready to look, feel and confidently offer my true self to the world!"

"Toi's impeccable vision and care for me as an individual left me wanting to recommend her services and expertise to anyone who wants to represent their personality and message with an authentic relevancy."

Now that you've seen everything come together for Andrea, isn't it time to try it for yourself?

CHAPTER NINE

PRACTICE MAKES BETTER

WHATEVER IT IS THAT YOU GET TO DO EVERY MORNING, DO IT IN A WAY THAT HONORS YOUR TEAM, YOUR CRAFT, AND YOUR INDUSTRY.

You are now thinking about your personal brand in a different way.

Your personal brand is both an internal and external process. If affects what you do and say, and the impressions you make both online and off. It takes practice—10,000 hours, to be exact. Practice the tools that you have learned in this book, because practice makes things easier.

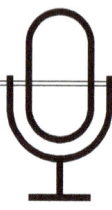

INTERVIEW

MARCUS ALLEN

CEO OF **BIG BROTHERS, BIG SISTERS**

"PRACTICE DOES NOT MAKE PERFECT; PRACTICE MAKES BETTER." —MARCUS ALLEN

WHY IS PRACTICING SOMETHING IMPORTANT?

Practice doesn't make perfect, right? Practice makes better. And so, you have to continue to practice. No matter how you slice it, we're always competing with something or someone.

2% of people in this world are real leaders. There's

a small percentage of athletes that actually go on to play professional ball or professional sports. There's a small percentage of people who actually go into C suite level positions, a small percentage of people who actually go on to boards, a small percentage of people actually become millionaires, a small percentage of people who actually have successful marriages, right? You have to understand that there is a discipline that they had to implement to do that, and it was work. It was practice.

Let's take marriage, for instance. When you have a series of failures, they make you better. I've been divorced twice, so I know a little bit of what I'm talking about. Marriage is really similar to a career or any sport. Marriage is only going to be as good as the work that you put into it.

People think that you just get married to somebody. They think it just happens, like, "I love her, she loves me. And this is going to be great." But it's not sustainable.

You have to have two people who are really focused on the work, right?

When I hear people say, "Well, it shouldn't be that hard, it shouldn't be that much work to make a marriage work."

To those people, I say, "Well, you should keep reading those fiction books, right?"

We all grow. And we all grow in different ways. If we're not constantly communicating and working on each other, working on ourselves, and working on our environment, then at some point our lives are going to get fractured.

We have to understand that we weren't put here on this earth to be lazy, and for things to just come to us easily. I believe we were put here to be learning, developing beings. And if that is true, then we have to look at how it applies to every aspect of our life.

You don't stay in shape, without working out. Right? You don't get smarter without reading. Right? Employees don't produce without training. Right?

Nothing in our lives tells us or shows us that we don't have to work at it. It's that combination of putting yourself in the right frame of mind, regardless of what's happening, giving yourself the motivation to keep going forward, and the work ethic to say no matter what, I'm going to keep my feet moving forward.

"You earn your trophies at practice. You just pick them up at the competitions."

— - UNKNOWN

When we apply that quote to becoming a well-dressed brand, we could say: "You earn your trophies in your closet. You just pick them up when your brand crushes it in the game!"

IT'S TIME TO SHUT IT DOWN!

I hope that I have encouraged you to be your own total package! Your own kind of beautiful. Show up and shut it down!

Whatever it is that you get to do every morning, do it in a way that honors your team, your craft, and your industry. I only ask that you look good while doing it!

"Dressing well is a form of good manners."

— - TOM FORD, DESIGNER

When I think about this quote, it reminds me of the story of Esther in the Bible. Esther could not just roll out of bed and go running to the king!

Before an eligible young woman could go before the king, she was prescribed 12 months of beauty treatments (*Esther 2:12*). But Esther was beautiful, both inside and out. She was strong, brave, and confident. She was a total package.

Image is important because we are made in the image of God. In fact, your personal brand began before you were even born. As you were knitted together in your mother's womb, God's hands were guiding you.

My friend Jim Bracelin, Vice President of the Sign Language Institute of America, had some insight to share about being made in the image of God. Check out the interview on the following page.

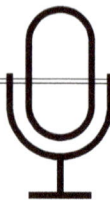

INTERVIEW

JIM BRACELIN

VICE PRESIDENT OF **THE SIGN LANGUAGE INSTITUTE OF AMERICA**

"GOD CREATED US WITH VALUE. IT'S AS THOUGH GOD GAVE EACH OF US INDIVIDUALLY, SPECIFICALLY A PURPOSEFUL BRAND." —JIM BRACELIN

WHAT DOES IT MEAN TO BE "MADE IN THE IMAGE OF GOD?"

As we think about branding, we think about the image we pose to other people that we display to other people. We spend a lot of time on that. We spend a lot of time making sure that what we do with the outside of us is acceptable to the people we will be around that day. As we start our day, we begin thinking, "Who am I going to see today? What do I need to do today? Who will I be in front of? Is this appropriate or not appropriate?" We spend a lot of time thinking about how we appear to other people. But the bottom line is that God created us, each of us in His image.

The Bible says, "So God created man in His own image." (*Genesis 1:27*)

When we think about that, does that mean that God has hair like mine and yours? No, that's not what it's talking about at all. We're so focused on the external, but God focuses on the internal.

When he was choosing the king for Israel, God told the prophet, "Don't only look at what you see on the outside, but look at what's on the inside of this person." (*1 Samuel 16:7*)

When we think about God creating us in His own image, that's a pretty awesome thought. Matter of fact, that makes all of us extremely valuable.

No matter how successful you are or how important your title may be, you may still wonder, does anybody even know I exist? Am I important, even in the least, to anybody?

We may have these feelings of depression. We may get feelings of low self-worth. We may be scratching the bottom. We may look successful on the outside in the eyes of those around us. And yet, on the inside, we're suffering. We feel a lack of importance. We experience a lack of value. But the fact that God created us in His own image is an incredible thought.

The word "image" in that verse doesn't mean that we are small gods. It doesn't mean that we have the right to make our own choices without any repercussions because we are the ones who run the universe. It's not talking about that at all. The word "image" literally means "like a reflection."

Maine is one of my favorite states, with beautiful mountainsides, wooded areas, and wonderful lakes.

The lakes are still, with the mountains going up either side. I've been driving down the road and looked across a lake, seeing the forest that goes up from it. I can't tell where the shore begins, because the reflection of the trees in the forest is absolutely perfect on the water. The reflection on the water is not trees; it's simply a reflection.

That's the picture of God creating us in His image. We're not God. But He created us after his own character, after his own personality. He's got emotion, He has will, and He's got decision making processes. And He made us that way as well. He created us with value. It's as though God gave each of us individually, specifically a purposeful brand.

The problem is that we've failed the brand that God gave us. The Bible calls it sin. We've just messed up.

You may dress up and leave the house perfect, with everything in order in that morning. And then the rain comes. Your hair flops and your clothes are wet, and you're wrinkled. And you think, "Oh, what am I going to do today?"

That's what happens with us with our relationship with God. When sin came into the world, our brand was marred. Our image was tarnished. His reflection on us that should be clear as crystal was now blurred and hard to see. As we go through our lives, the further we go in sin, the more distorted that brand becomes.

If I have an outdated suit, it just gets moved to the back of the closet. I ignore it. Maybe I'll give it away to Goodwill. But I don't use it anymore. I don't wear it anymore. God could have easily done that with each of us because we failed. We have failed in significant ways and we continue to fail.

God could have thrown us off to the side, put us on the shelf, and said, "No more. I'm not going to care about that person anymore." But that's never what God does.

The Bible says very simply, and pointedly, God is

love. God, while we were in the condition with the marred image, with the brand we almost destroyed, He looked down at us and said, "You know, I can't take that those people are not my people. So, I'm going to do all it takes on my part, to restore the brand, to restore the relationship, to give that image a new start". And so, God sent His one and only Son, Jesus Christ, leaving heaven to come here to a sin-cursed earth.

Jesus lived here for 33 years. Now he had a great life, yet he was without sin. There were a lot of people that loved him. But there were also a lot of people that hated him.

One day, Jesus Christ went to the cross of Calvary. I know you've heard this story before. Many people have heard it; they just dismiss it. "Oh, yeah, Jesus went to the cross." But it's far more than that. Jesus Christ came to this earth to restore the image.

Jesus Christ came to earth as the only perfect human being, who could take on this responsibility. We may think, "Oh, if I'm religious, that will restore the image." But religion doesn't restore the image. That's another external attempt to fix an internal image in us; and it cannot be done. Religion cannot fix it. No good deed can fix it.

We're the ones that caused the damage, so we can't restore it. But God in heaven reached out with Jesus Christ. Jesus died on the cross. The Bible tells us that Jesus took the marred image with us to the grave with him, conquered that marred image in the grave, conquered our sin, conquered our own death, and conquered the enemy. Then he rose from the grave on the first day of the week.

Now there be many people that say, "Well, I don't know if I believe that." Frankly, it is a matter of faith. You have to have faith to believe this. But it's your choice. Each person has that unique image of God in each of us that is different from everyone else. No two people are the same. Even identical twins are different. In his great infinite love, God has a plan that's uniquely designed for each of us individually, not for just the general populace.

The Bible tells us not only did Jesus rise from the dead, but over 500 people saw him alive after he had been crucified. He was not a ghost; he was not a spirit. After he rose from the dead, people touched him, ate with him, and drank with him. They were able to talk with him.

Jesus Christ died, was buried, and rose from the grave. Believing in Jesus is a personal decision. God made us personally individually in his image. We marred that image when we sinned. But God offers restitution of that image. God offers a renewal of that original image that he placed within us. And He does it through his one and only son, Jesus.

The bottom line today comes to this point: without Jesus Christ, your life has no peace. Your life has no lasting joy. Your life has no lasting satisfaction.

We're living in a surface world that tries to recreate a new surface that will somehow impact the depth of our soul. It doesn't work that way.

Everybody searches for love. We can't find it in this world. We try one relationship that fails, so we go to another one. We try this new car or that new house or that new outfit, we go through all of these things, and yet nothing satisfies. I'll tell you why: because that original image has not been restored.

We can only be satisfied, we can only have peace, and we can only have that true lasting love when we embrace the One who made us, to begin with, to receive the gift of restoration.

Would you consider having the image of God restored in you today? Would you receive the gift that God already purchased for you? It's not something you can buy; it's not something you can earn. God says it's already been done. God has created for you an eternal life that will restore the image that He created in you from the very beginning of time.

If you can take just a moment where you are, pray this simple prayer, "Dear Jesus, I know that I'm a sinner. I believe that you came to this earth and lived here without sin, went to the cross, and died on the cross. I believe you were buried and you rose from the grave to restore me. I trust you and only you to forgive my sin and give me a home in heaven."

If you prayed that prayer, and you really meant business, I want to tell you right now, the image that was marred within you has been restored. God wants to do a great work in you from this point forward. God wants to restore a relationship with you that will continue throughout eternity.

The image that God made within you will be on display. Your brand has been renewed; it's been restored. God can transform you into the kind of person that you've always wanted to be. Along with that gift you received comes peace, love, and joy. You'll still have troubles, you'll still have problems, but now you walk with your heavenly Creator. God has the opportunity to help you where you cannot help yourself.

You are special! You are unique. You are already enough; your brand allows you to be more of who you are.

You are fearfully and wonderfully made. (Psalm 139:14). Now it's time to own it.

> "Your personal style is your logo. Your personality is your brand promise. Being unique is how you add value. Dominating your niche is your trademark. Packaging this in a way that blows people's minds is your personal brand."
>
> — - TOI SWEENEY

Your brand starts at the core and root of who you are. If the root of the tree is nourished, the tree will bear much fruit.

You are the apple of God's eye—today, tomorrow, and the next day! Wake up, be awesome, and show the world your well-dressed brand.

TOI SWEENEY

CEO OF **THE WELL DRESSED BRAND**

STYLE QUIZ

The purpose of your image is to maximize the impact of your nonverbal communications. Your image should reflect the likeness of your personal brand; It includes all of your visual marketing collateral, from your logo to your social media profiles, and even includes what you choose to wear.

It's important for you to have a strong visual identity across the board. You are your brand's persona and the face of your brand.

How do you know if you need help with your image? I'm not going to tell you to ask your friends, because they love you and will not tell you the truth. So, instead ... think about your wardrobe for a second.

When was the last time you updated your look? What about your clothing? Have you been wearing the same style and cut for the last 5 years, or are you making small updates each season to stay relevant?

I don't want you to settle for just looking "fine" or "ok", why would you settle for that? You should be remarkable, stunning, magnificent, and gorgeous.

"Your time as a caterpillar has expired. Your wings are ready."

— - TOI SWEENEY

WHAT'S YOUR UNIQUE STYLE IDENTITY?

Answer the questions below to pinpoint your unique style identity. Circle as many answers per question as you wish; your responses may vary based on your career look, your usual after-work attire, or even your dream style. Then, tally your answers at the bottom. Have fun!

WHAT CLOTHING STYLE ARE YOU DRAWN TO?

A. Offbeat and artistic

B. Bold and dramatic

C. Dainty and prim

D. Put-together and functional

E. Comfortable and uncomplicated

F. Minimalist and polished

WHAT DO YOU WEAR TO WORK?

A. Original pieces with an artistic flair

B. Striking, attention-getting outfits

C. Feminine tops with floral print or lace embellishments

D. Custom-fitted business suits

E. Mix-and-match, effortless pieces

F. Simple, elegant separates with chic jewelry

HOW WOULD YOU DESCRIBE YOUR OFF-DUTY STYLE?

A. Pieces by my favorite pioneering designer

B. High-end boutique styles

C. Flouncy, soft, ladylike outfits

D. Timeless pieces in neutral colors

E. A comfy shirt and jeans

F. Basic pieces in tonal colors

WHAT KIND OF COLORS DO YOU LIKE TO WEAR?

A. Any color, depending on my mood

B. Bold colors that pop

C. Soft, pretty colors, like blush, rose, ivory, etc.

D. Grays, beiges, and other neutral colors

E. Effortless, no-nonsense combinations

F. Elegant, monochromatic colors in varying hues (all black, ivory, navy, etc.)E. Mix-and-match, effortless pieces

F. Simple, elegant separates with chic jewelry

HOW DO YOU APPLY AND WEAR YOUR MAKEUP?

A. I love trying trendy colors & styles

B. I prefer striking, distinct lip and eye colors

C. I adore a soft, pretty, feminine look

D. I have a tried-and-true daily regimen with go-to basics

E. Less is more; I wear as little makeup as possible

F. I love makeup that coordinates well with my clothing

WHAT HAIRSTYLE FITS YOU BEST?

A. It depends on the day's look

B. I prefer dramatic styles that leave an impression

C. I like long, wavy locks or a loose updo

D. Professional and classic styles fit me best

E. I love a nice look that doesn't require a lot of work

F. I enjoy trying the latest hair trends

WHAT'S YOUR FAVORITE STYLE OF JEWELRY?

A. Artistic, one-of-a-kind pieces

B. Attention-grabbing and daring

C. Delicate, detailed, and feminine

D. Basic but beautiful

E. Small, light, comfortable pieces

F. Modern and elegant

IF YOU WERE A SHOE, WHAT KIND OF SHOE WOULD YOU BE?

A. Wildly stylish & unique

B. Stilettos or high heels

C. Ballet flats or low heels with pretty embellishments

D. Pumps that coordinate with my outfit

E. Super comfy flats or trainers

F. Short boots or fashionable flats

WHAT DO YOU WEAR TO A WEDDING?

A. A vintage designer dress with a combination of fabrics

B. A unique, fitted, eye-catching outfit

C. A flowing dress or gown with romantic details

D. A timeless, fitted dress with a classic touch

E. A soft, breathable blouse with comfy pants or a skirt

F. Sophisticated separates or a stylish gown

WHAT'S YOUR SHOPPING STYLE?

A. I'm a treasure hunter and love shopping off the beaten path

B. I purchase pieces that I feel will make a statement

C. I love the journey of searching for the perfect outfit

D. I keep shopping to a well-planned minimum

E. I only shop when I have to

F. I make large, carefully-considered clothing purchases

YOU'RE AT A LARGE GATHERING, LIKE A CONVENTION OR A PARTY. WHAT IMPRESSION DO YOU WANT TO MAKE?

A. I want people to see me as offbeat and intriguing

B. I want to stand out as a power player in my field, no matter where I am

C. I want to be appear attractive, sweet, and approachable

D. I want my well-planned attire to be a reflection of who I am: classic and practical

E. I want to blend in, with a chill, girl-next-door kind of vibe

F. I want to shine as a fashion-forward, sophisticated professional

RESULTS

After you've finished the quiz, tally your answers by letter. The letter you selected most often will determine your unique style identity. Then, find the description of your style identity, plus tips for getting a look that fits you best.

A _____

B _____

C _____

D _____

E _____

F _____

MOSTLY A - INNOVATIVE

You are *Innovative*! Creative and free-spirited, you love to experiment with inventive, artistic styles that are one step ahead of the trends. You're not afraid of color, and you enjoy combining unconventional patterns and textures to create a look that is all your own.

Treasure hunting for funky vintage finds at the thrift store is your jam, and you're the most likely of your friends to bring home an unusual piece of clothing or jewelry from your exotic vacation.

MOSTLY B - POWERFUL

You are *Powerful*! Daring, poised, and self-assured, your fashion choices perfectly mirror your strong personality. You love distinctive attire in vibrant colors, defined textures, and rich fabrics. Dressing in an outfit that is relevant to your surroundings—like a conference, special event, or girls' night out—gives you a thrill. You tend to choose pieces of clothing with striking features, like asymmetrical hemlines, dramatic sleeves, thigh-high boots, and statement accessories.

MOSTLY C - LADYLIKE

You are *Ladylike*! Romantic and demure, you love clothing with delicate details and charming, feminine patterns. You prefer muted, pastel hues and soft, flowing fabrics. Elegant embellishments, lace, sheer fabrics, and some floral prints tend to catch your eye.

Dainty, romantic pieces of jewelry are your go-to accessories. You're not afraid of a little flounce, and it's common for you to wear pieces accented with frills or ruffles.

MOSTLY D - TIMELESS

You are *Timeless*! Traditional and iconic, you prefer classic clothing styles that stand the test of time.

You love beautifully put-together looks with a traditional fit, and aren't concerned with following the latest fad.

When it comes to fashion, functionality is king, and your practical nature drives you to choose ageless pieces that you can wear for years to come. Clean, beautiful styles reminiscent of classic Hollywood are right up your alley.

MOSTLY E - EFFORTLESS

You are *Effortless*! Laid back and low-maintenance, you crave comfort over frills—every time. You love soft, non-restrictive mix-and-match pieces that can easily be dressed up or down with minimal fuss. From head to toe, you demand to feel comfortable; finish off your look with flats, sandals, fashion sneakers or wedges to keep your feet happy. If your outfits looks great for the office but also feel relaxing off-duty, you're there!

MOSTLY F - POLISHED

You are *Polished*! Chic and elegant, you love sophisticated, perfectly-tailored clothing. You always keep one finger on the pulse of the fashion industry, and you love to try the latest posh trends. Luxe fabrics in shades of black, white, ivory, and gray are tried-and-true choices you'll revisit again and again.

You prefer a minimalist approach to fashion, and tend to view your carefully-considered clothing purchases as investments.

AFTERWORD

Hey Friends!

Thank you for purchasing my book. It's hard to believe that I wrote the first edition five years ago. Thank you for being so supportive of my hopes, ideas, and dreams. I love you.

Many things, thoughts, and ideas have changed around the world over the last five years. I've made every effort to update this body of work. I am not perfect, so if you read something that I may have missed that does not fit into how we move through the world today, my only request is that you extend me some grace.

I stand strong in my faith and the assignment I was given when I wrote this book. I am humbled and grateful that this book has helped so many. I pray that you will be blessed as you read it. I pray God's favor on you and all that you are trying to achieve in your life.

May you do it as a *Well Dressed Brand*.

Tori Sweeney

ACKNOWLEDGEMENTS

This book is dedicated to my loving Father, from whom all my blessing flow. My heavenly Father, who, despite all the ways I should have been in heaven, He saw fit to plant dreams in my heart and stars in my eyes and tell me every day that He loves me and believes in me. He told me so much and wrote it across my heart with his blood until I started to believe it. Thank you, Father God.

To Dr. Elisa Ross, whose name I cannot say without crying. Thank you for saving my life when we lost our son, Miles Jackson Sweeney, due to a uterine rupture. Thank you for carefully removing our son from my body so that I did not have the same fate. Without you and the grace of

God, this book would not be possible. Thank you for being more than the greatest surgeon and girl boss, wife, and friend. Thank you for doing your job so well that I get to live! I will never let your work be in vain. I will move forward as long as it is the Lord's plan.

To my exceptional sister-in-law, Karen. Thank you for carrying Tucker for me so that I get to be a mom. I can't imagine my life without his beautiful brown eyes and dimples. He is pretty special in so many ways. Only once in a lifetime could someone offer to carry your child for you without wanting anything in return. You are forever my greatest love and his. The bond that the two of you have is magical. Thank you for being a source of joy in my life. I love you.

To John and Tucker Sweeney! Thank you for all your love, support, and prayers. Thank you for cheering me on as I learn to fly. You are my everything.

ACKNOWLEDGEMENTS

And a special thank you to all my friends, family, and church family for your donations to my Go-Fund Me, your prayers, text messages, phone calls, and Facebook posts. I can't even believe we did this!"

SWEENEY FAMILY
BLACK LIGHT RUN 2019

ABOUT THE AUTHOR

TOI SWEENEY

FOUNDER AND CHIEF STYLE OFFICER
THE WELL DRESSED BRAND

Toi Sweeney is an award-winning fashion stylist, brand image strategist, speaker, entrepreneur, author of *Secrets of a Well-Dressed Brand*, founder of the Well Dressed Brand, and host of Well Dressed Brand TV.

Toi helps powerhouse brands and high-performers integrate their wardrobes into their business plans through a stunning, distinctive style that clearly communicates their highest value. She's passionate about leveraging her Fascination Advantage™ training and the psychology of color to develop signature styles for her clients that help them show up and shut it down.

Toi has been featured on Forbes.com, BBCNews.com, HelloGiggles.com, and has appeared as a guest on over three dozen podcasts. She has two decades of extensive experience in fashion, business, and marketing, and her clients have a appeared on The Today Show, Harry, Fox, ABC, NBC, QVC, The Hallmark Channel, and Anderson Cooper Live. Toi is also a recipient of the prestigious Telly Award and a recipient of the Icon of the Year award via the Art Institute.

CONNECT WITH TOI

 @TOISWEENEY

 TOISWEENEY.COM

 TOI.SWEENEY@GMAIL.COM

www.ingramcontent.com/pod-product-compliance
Lightning Source LLC
Chambersburg PA
CBHW051622010526
44119CB00039B/479/J